Mapping Global Issues

Poverty and Hunger

Cath Senker

W

FRANKLIN WATTS
LONDON · SYDNEY

First published in 2011 by Franklin Watts
Copyright © 2011 Arcturus Publishing Limited

Franklin Watts
338 Euston Road
London NW1 3BH

Franklin Watts Australia
Level 17/207 Kent Street, Sydney, NSW 2000

Produced by Arcturus Publishing Limited, 26/27 Bickels Yard, 151–153 Bermondsey Street, London SE1 3HA

The right of Cath Senker to be identified as the author of this work has been asserted by her in accordance with the Copyright, Designs and Patents Act 1988.

Series concept: Alex Woolf   Editor and picture researcher: Alex Woolf
Designer: Jane Hawkins   Map illustrator: Stefan Chabluk

Picture credits: Corbis: 7 (Earl & Nazima Kowall), cover and 11 (Finbarr O'Reilly/Reuters), 14 (Andy Aitchison/In Pictures), 18 (Divyakant Solanki/epa), 22 (Philippe Lissac/Godong), 27 (Thomas Hartwell), 30 (Viviane Moos), 35 (Manca Juvan/In Pictures), 39 (epa), 41 (Louise Gubb), 43 (Parth Sanyal/Reuters). Shutterstock: 23 (thefinalmiracle), 31 (Frontpage), 34 (Elena Rostunova).

Every attempt has been made to clear copyright. Should there be any inadvertent omission, please apply to the publisher for rectification.

Cover picture: A mother with her malnourished baby, during a severe food crisis in Niger.

The author would like to acknowledge the following sources for the panels and quotations: 6–7: European Anti-Poverty Network; 10–11: Africa News 8 Jul 2010; 12–13: From 'Local Voices: A Community Perspective on HIV and Hunger in Zambia' ACF/CINDI Kitwe, 2007; 8–19: Banwari from Childhood Poverty Research and Policy Centre; 20–21: 'India: working on the front line, Madhuri Dass, Save the Children 4 Feb 2008; 22–3: 'Livestock a lifeline for Pakistan's women' Department For International Development website, 16 Jun 2009; 24–5: 'Progress toward Millennium Development Goals in the Middle East and North Africa', Farzaneh Roudi-Fahimi, Population Reference Bureau, 2004; 26–7: Student Voices, American Language Center, Rabat, Morocco; 28–9: 'Bitter lives of Bolivia's child workers' Andres Schipani, BBC News, 11 Oct 2009; 32–3: 'Bolsa Família: Changing the Lives of Millions in Brazil', The World Bank, 2010; 34–5: 'Romani children denied proper education in Slovakia', Amnesty International, 24 Apr 2009; 38–9: Matthew Pennycook 'Not Just For the Good Times: The New Imperative for Fair Pay', Fair Pay Network, 2009; 42–3: 'Climate Change Adaptation in Practice', Oxfam, Nov 2009.

Map sources: 9: based on figures from the UN Statistics Division; 13: FAO; 17: Project Ploughshares; 20: UN World Food Programme; 25: based on figures from the CIA World Factbook; 29: US Census Bureau, American Commmunity Survey, 2009; and Puerto Rico Community Survey, 2009; 32: UN World Food Programme; 37: World Bank Millennium Development Goals, 2005.

A CIP catalogue record for this book is available from the British Library.

Dewey Decimal Classification Number: 338.1'9

ISBN 978 1 4451 0515 4
SL001636EN
Supplier 03, Date 0911, Print Run 1039

Printed in China

Franklin Watts is a division of Hachette Children's Books, an Hachette UK company.
www.hachette.co.uk

Contents

1: Introduction

In 2005 an estimated 1.4 billion people, mostly in the developing world, were eking out a living in extreme poverty – that's about one-quarter of the global population. In 2008, nearly one-fifth of people in developing countries went hungry. With all the wealth, technology and scientific advances in the world, why are so many people poor? This chapter defines poverty and hunger and examines why they occur.

What is poverty?

The cost of living varies in different countries, so an international poverty line is used to compare poverty rates. People who earn less than US$1.25 a day are defined as living in absolute poverty. They do not have enough money for basic needs such as food and shelter. The highest rates of absolute poverty are in sub-Saharan Africa and South Asia, and 70 per cent of the world's poorest people are female.

Relative poverty is when you are poor compared to the people around you, for example, if you live in the United States and cannot afford a car. Unemployed people, temporary workers and the elderly often suffer from relative poverty.

An alternative measure is human poverty, which includes non-material aspects. People in human poverty are not only short of money – they lack a sense of dignity, may not feel part of a community and have little power to control their lives. As one European in poverty says: 'The way people look at you is humiliating. You are not considered a human being.'

FACTS and FIGURES

PEOPLE IN ABSOLUTE POVERTY

The percentage of people living on less than US$1.25 a day in 2005:

Sub-Saharan Africa	51
South Asia	39
South-East Asia	19
East Asia	16
Latin America and the Caribbean	8
Western Asia	6
Commonwealth of Independent States	5
North Africa	3
Transition countries of south-eastern Europe	1

Source: MDG Report, 2010

What causes poverty?

There is poverty in all countries because of inequality. Not everyone benefits equally from economic growth. Overall, the European Union (EU) is wealthy, but nearly one in seven people is at risk of poverty. The high level of poverty in developing countries has mainly historical reasons. Between the 16th and 20th centuries, European countries ruled most Latin American, Asian and African countries as colonies. They exploited their resources and prevented them from industrializing. The economic divide between rich and poor nations continued to grow after the colonies became independent.

Since the 1980s, countries have become increasingly interdependent through globalization – the growth of international trade, communications, travel and culture. Transnational companies (TNCs) have become the main traders in the world economy. Countries have been forced to open

Children scrabble through piles of rubbish in Calcutta, India, in an attempt to find edible food or objects they can sell.

up their economies to greater international trade. The TNCs bargain for the lowest prices for products. Local producers have to compete with their counterparts in other countries and sell their products as cheaply as possible. The prices of agricultural goods, mostly grown in developing countries, have fallen dramatically. Since their income is so low, millions of farmers are in poverty.

Hunger – the facts

The number of hungry people worldwide leapt from 842 million in 1990–92 to

FACTS and FIGURES

FACTORS INFLUENCING HUNGER

In her 1987 book, *The Hunger Machine*, poverty expert and campaigner Susan George listed six factors that influence who goes hungry. Race and disability could be added to the list.

1. North–South divide: the countries of the South tend to be poorer.

2. The division between developing and developed countries.

3. The rural–urban divide: there tends to be more poverty in rural areas.

4. Social class: working-class people are poorer than the middle or upper class.

5. Gender: women make up 70% of the world's poor.

6. Age: retired people are more likely to be in poverty.

1.2 billion during 2009 – the highest number ever. In 2008 the global economic crisis led to lower incomes and higher unemployment, yet food prices rose. So hunger increased. Children in particular suffer from hunger. One-quarter of children in developing regions are underweight for their age. Children who go hungry do not grow properly and run a greater risk of dying before adulthood.

Why do people go hungry?

Although globalization has led to a huge expansion in food production, more people are malnourished. Some experts blame the rising population of poor countries for the growth in hunger. The world's population has soared, especially in developing countries, growing from 5.3 billion in 1990 to 6.8 billion in 2009.

Others point to the way food is produced. In the past, farmers practised subsistence agriculture, growing food for their family and community. Over the past half a century they have shifted to producing mostly cash crops to sell. As subsistence agriculture has declined, people can eat only if they can afford to buy food. In developing countries, poor people spend up to 80 per cent of their income on food.

The unequal distribution of food is another factor. The United Nations Food and Agriculture Organization (FAO) estimates that there is enough grain to provide everyone in the world with 3,600

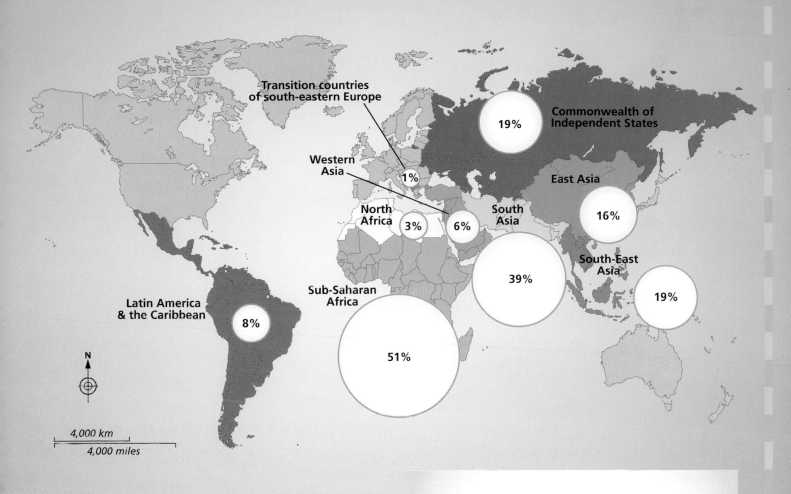

Transition countries
of south-eastern Europe

1%

Commonwealth of
Independent States

19%

Western
Asia

North
Africa

3%

6%

South
Asia

39%

East Asia

16%

South-East
Asia

19%

Latin America
& the Caribbean

8%

Sub-Saharan
Africa

51%

N

4,000 km

4,000 miles

This map indicates the percentage of people surviving on less than US$1.25 a day in different regions of the world. Each region appears in a different colour.

calories a day – that's 1,200 more than the recommended minimum daily intake. However, developing countries produce the majority of the world's food and people in developed countries eat most of it! They consume far more per person.

What is being done?

In 2000 the Millennium Declaration set 2015 as the target date to achieve the Millennium Development Goals (MDGs). Goal One was to halve the proportion of people whose income is less than US$1

a day (updated in 2008 to US$1.25) and to halve the proportion of hungry people. In 2010 many areas of the developing world were on track to meet the poverty reduction goal, but the number of hungry people was growing. This book examines these challenges in the different regions of the world and what is being done to alleviate poverty and hunger.

2: Sub-Saharan Africa

In sub-Saharan Africa (the area of the continent south of the Sahara), progress towards reducing poverty and hunger greatly lags behind all other regions of the world. From 1990 to 2005, the percentage of people living on US$1.25 fell slightly from 58 to 51 per cent. In other words, half of Africa's population still exists in extreme poverty. The proportion of hungry people declined in the mid-2000s but started to increase again during the 2008 economic crisis, which led to a rise in the price of basic foodstuffs and imported food.

Where are hunger and poverty worst?

The entire region suffers from extreme poverty, especially in areas of conflict. For example, in 2010, conflict raged in the eastern region of the Democratic Republic of Congo (DRC), the Darfur region of Sudan and the Niger Delta in Nigeria. Countries recovering from conflict, such as Sierra Leone, Liberia and the Central African Republic, struggled to feed their people. Poverty is also a particular problem for landlocked countries (with no access to the sea), as it is costly for such countries to transport goods to and from the coast for international trade. In 2010 the landlocked nation of Chad was on the brink of a food catastrophe. In 2009 about 265 million Africans were undernourished, the majority of them in Eastern and Central Africa. In

2010 Africa's Sahel region in West and Central Africa experienced hunger owing to the failure of the rains the previous year and poor harvests. By June, 10 million were at risk of starvation in Niger, Chad, Mali,

FACTS and FIGURES

HUNGER IN AFRICA

• Every minute, 12 people in Africa die from malnutrition.

• 1 in 4 people on the continent are undernourished.

• In Malawi, 44% of the population are undernourished.

• In Niger, nearly 17% of children under 5 are suffering from acute malnutrition.

Source: Global Alliance for Improved Nutrition, 2010

This mother and her baby are victims of a severe food crisis in Niger. The baby's red bracelet indicates that she is extremely malnourished.

Mauritania and Burkina Faso. In the worst-hit areas, families sold their livestock to buy food, took their children out of school and migrated to cities in search of work.

Reasons for poverty: unfair trade

Unfair trade is a significant reason for the desperate poverty of many Africans. Since the 1980s, most African countries have had to allow other countries to sell them goods. In developed countries, governments offer farmers subsidies to make their goods cheaper to export. Yet poor countries are prevented by world trade rules from giving subsidies to their own farmers, so their goods are more expensive than imports. For example, cheap, subsidized US cotton is sold in West Africa, putting local cotton farmers out of business.

Debt

National debt is another serious problem. The majority of the world's most heavily indebted countries are in sub-Saharan Africa. These countries fell into debt in the

1960s and 1970s when they borrowed money to finance development projects. Then, in the 1980s, interest rates rose and the debts increased rapidly. African governments have to spend a huge proportion of their national budget on paying off debt, leaving less money available to spend on health and education – services that are essential to reduce poverty.

Ill-health

Health and poverty are closely linked. People living in extremely rundown areas are prone to illness. For example, in the vast urban slums of Kenya, there is no clean water supply. Dirty water is a major cause of disease. When poor people fall sick, they often cannot afford treatment. While unwell, they are unable to work and can slip deeper into poverty.

Serious diseases have brought about a health catastrophe in sub-Saharan Africa. It is not just the poor who catch these diseases, but they are the least able to afford treatment. Malaria led to nearly 863,000 deaths in 2008, while HIV/AIDS causes the early death of millions. The worst-affected countries are Zambia, Zimbabwe, Swaziland, the Central African Republic and Lesotho. In 2010 a baby born in Zambia could expect to live just 39 years.

Lack of education

Education is as necessary as health as a means of enabling people to break out of the cycle of poverty. Many children who cannot go to school are aware that education could improve their opportunities in later life. As 13-year-old Sofia from Tanzania says: 'I know if I go to school, one day I will be able to help my family as I will get a good job that pays well.' There have been some improvements in the number of sub-Saharan African children who complete primary school. In 2008, 76 per cent were enrolled in primary education, up from 58 per cent in 1999. Yet education for all was still a long way off.

PERSPECTIVES

IVY'S ORPHAN FAMILY

Ivy is 19 and lives in Zambia. Since her parents died of disease, she has had to support herself and four younger siblings. She receives aid from the charity CINDI Kitwe.

When things are okay we eat every day using 'maize meal', which is given to me by a community-based organization because we are orphans that live on our own. I stretch it out and cook it with pumpkin or sweet potato leaves instead of vegetables, but if the 'maize meal' runs out I have to buy food for the house.

We have an uncle who is still alive and he donates money to me that I use to buy food. I try not to rely on him because he has a lot of children and other dependants to look after, so when things get really difficult I take my brothers and sister to the maize hammer mill and we collect the left-over residuals of maize that I sieve and cook.

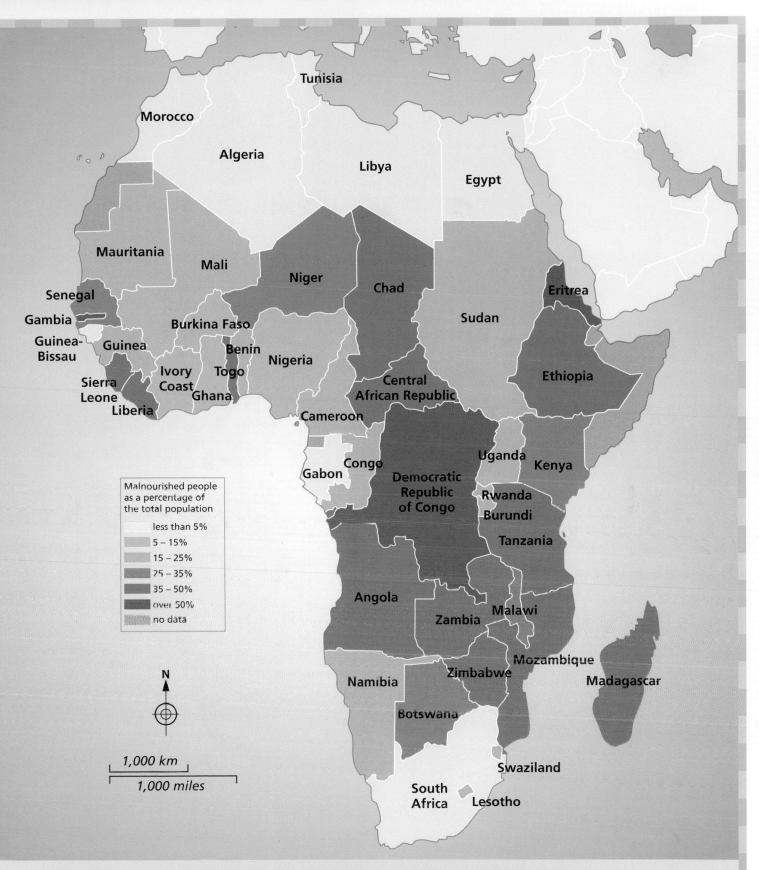

Malnourished people as a percentage of the total population

- less than 5%
- 5 – 15%
- 15 – 25%
- 25 – 35%
- 35 – 50%
- over 50%
- no data

N

1,000 km

1,000 miles

Tunisia
Morocco
Algeria
Libya
Egypt
Mauritania
Mali
Niger
Chad
Sudan
Eritrea
Senegal
Gambia
Guinea-Bissau
Guinea
Burkina Faso
Benin
Nigeria
Central African Republic
Ethiopia
Sierra Leone
Ivory Coast
Togo
Ghana
Liberia
Cameroon
Gabon
Congo
Democratic Republic of Congo
Uganda
Kenya
Rwanda
Burundi
Tanzania
Angola
Zambia
Malawi
Namibia
Zimbabwe
Mozambique
Madagascar
Botswana
Swaziland
South Africa
Lesotho

This map indicates the percentage of people who are malnourished in African countries. It has been shown that a single year of primary school increases the wages people earn later in life by 5 to 15 per cent for boys, and even more for girls.

13

Patrick Kajjura picks coffee beans from his farm in Kamuli region, Uganda. Uganda has many fairtrade coffee producers whose quality of life has been improved by their involvement in the scheme.

Solving poverty: aid and debt

What can be done to improve the dire situation of many Africans? In 2005 the wealthy countries reaffirmed a pledge to give 0.7 per cent of their national incomes in aid, although only a few countries, such as Denmark and Norway, have fulfilled their promise. The aid provided has had some positive effects, such as increasing access to health care and education, and supplying HIV medication. However, organizations such as Oxfam have pointed out that it is vital to ensure that aid is effective (see panel).

Aid cannot solve all the problems though. The poorest countries are saddled with huge debts. Schemes such as the Multilateral Debt Relief Initiative offer debt relief (reduction) to the most indebted countries, which are mostly in sub-Saharan Africa. Yet although some debt was cancelled in 2008–9, the poorest countries had to borrow more money because of the economic crisis.

Assisting farmers

On a smaller scale, introducing new farming techniques can decrease poverty and hunger. For example, fertilizers improve the productivity of the land. Farmers in Tigray, Ethiopia, manage a composting scheme to enrich the soil. Improved seeds are useful too. A 'new rice for Africa' (NERICA) has been developed – a cross between Asian and Africa rice varieties that is suited to drought conditions where farmers are unable to irrigate and cannot afford fertilizers. The rice matures in just three months and gives higher yields than traditional types. It has been adopted in countries such as Uganda, Ghana and Gambia.

The Fairtrade movement makes a contribution as well. Under a fairtrade agreement, a company offers to pay a higher price than the market rate for agricultural products such as coffee or cocoa over a long term. This provides a secure, fixed income for the grower. All of these schemes are useful, but unless the major issues of trade and debt are resolved, many sub-Saharan Africans will remain poor and hungry.

PERSPECTIVES

MAKING AID WORK

The campaigning organization Oxfam argues that aid could be made more effective:

It should no longer be conditional on recipients [receiving countries] promising economic change like privatizing or deregulating their services, cutting health and education spending, or opening up their markets. Aid should support poor countries' and communities' own plans and paths out of poverty.

At the same time, recipient countries need to have people and policies in place so that the aid is used in an honest and transparent way....

Aid also needs to focus better on poor people's needs. This means more aid being spent on areas such as basic health care and education.

Oxfam website, 2010

3: The Asia-Pacific Region

The Asia-Pacific region includes South, South-East and East Asia, as well as Oceania. It is home to 68 per cent of the world's people in extreme poverty. The highest levels of poverty and hunger are found in South Asia. In East Asia, the rapid economic development of the 'Asian Tigers' – South Korea, Malaysia, Taiwan, China, Hong Kong and Singapore – has helped lift many out of poverty. Poverty has also declined significantly in India. In the developed countries of Oceania, inequality has left pockets of poverty.

Which countries suffer most?

Despite improvements, India still suffers from high poverty and malnutrition rates. Nearly half of child deaths in India are due to hunger. Other countries with serious problems include Afghanistan, Bangladesh and Nepal. Afghanistan has experienced invasion, occupation (takeover by military forces) and civil war since 1979, all of which have damaged its economy. Afghans have had to rely on social networks, remittances (money sent from family members abroad) and the cultivation of drought-resistant crops. In rural areas, people survive by eating mostly cereals and they lack the nutrients provided by a more varied diet.

Bangladesh is one of the poorest and most densely populated countries in the world. Poverty is severest in cities and in five rural areas, where people endure

monga – 'hunger months' from September to November each year when the previous season's food runs out but the new crops

FACTS and FIGURES

POVERTY IN THE ASIA-PACIFIC REGION

The Asia-Pacific region has a large share of the developing world's deprived people. Percentage of the world's people:

Living below US$1.25 a day	68
Without basic sanitation (toilets and sewerage systems), rural areas	74
Without basic sanitation, urban areas	66
Under-5 underweight	71
Under-5 mortality	44

Source: Asia-Pacific Regional MDG Report 2009/10

have not yet been harvested. In Nepal, around a quarter of the population own no land, and nearly half are underemployed – they have work, but not enough to make a decent living.

Rural poverty

Generally, people in rural areas are far more likely to be in poverty than people in towns and cities. In Nepal, for instance, poverty overwhelmingly affects farmers – over 90 per cent of the poor live in the countryside. Most rural people rely on farming. The most common problem is not owning land or having limited access to land. Poor families often have several children to feed. If there

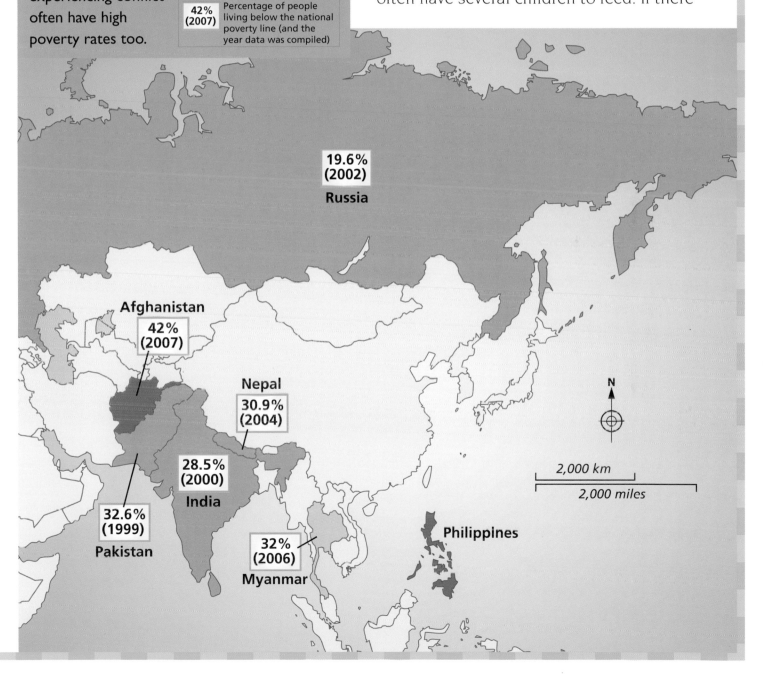

This map of the Asia-Pacific region shows that countries experiencing conflict often have high poverty rates too.

Civilian and military deaths in current phase of armed conflict
- 1,000 – 10,000
- 10,000 – 100,000
- over 100,000

42% (2007) Percentage of people living below the national poverty line (and the year data was compiled)

19.6% (2002)
Russia

Afghanistan
42% (2007)

Nepal
30.9% (2004)

28.5% (2000)
India

32.6% (1999)
Pakistan

32% (2006)
Myanmar

Philippines

N

2,000 km
2,000 miles

is a bad harvest, their income drops and they go hungry. In urban areas there are greater possibilities for casual work, such as street-trading, selling food, construction work or domestic service. There are more facilities such as schools and clinics to support the inhabitants. It is easier to scrape a living.

Survival on society's margins

As well as rural dwellers, groups on the margins of society, such as migrants, ethnic minorities and the disabled, are liable

Labourers dig the road in Mumbai, India. Generally, such workers are low paid and there are few safety precautions to protect them from injury.

to face poverty. In India, members of the Scheduled Tribes and Castes suffer greatly. Historically, Indian society was divided into four main castes, or social classes. The Scheduled Castes formed the bottom rung of the ladder. Enduring the lowest status in society, they did the menial, dirty, dangerous and badly paid jobs.

Although in Indian law it is illegal to discriminate on the grounds of caste, people of low caste still tend to work as unskilled labourers in small factories, building sites and mines, or sweeping the streets and clearing rubbish in cities. For instance, 17-year-old Banwari, from a Scheduled Caste in Tonk district, Rajasthan, works as a carpet-weaver for eight hours a day, which is tiring and unhealthy. As he says: 'My knees ache after long hours of sitting at the loom. Besides, the dust generated during weaving is harmful for the lungs and my eyes become strained and watery.' Many Scheduled Caste labourers work on a casual basis; some days they may not find any work at all. So they live with constant exhaustion, insecurity and a lack of funds.

Women

Women and children from the Scheduled Castes undertake the same kinds of jobs as men but for even lower wages. In general, across the region, women form the majority of unskilled, low-waged, temporary workers. They make up nearly two-thirds of migrant labourers, working on a casual basis in the

PERSPECTIVES

POVERTY DURING AN ECONOMIC CRISIS

When there is an economic crisis, it has a particularly severe effect on poor people:

The global economic crisis threatens to become a human crisis in many developing countries unless they can take targeted measures to protect vulnerable people in their communities.... While much of the world is focused on bank rescues and stimulus packages [to stimulate the economy], we should not forget that poor people in developing countries are far more exposed if their economies falter. This is a global crisis requiring a global solution. The needs of poor people in developing countries must be on the table.

World Bank President Robert B. Zoellick, 2009

most unpleasant jobs. When an economic crisis hits, such women are the first to be laid off.

Poverty amid plenty

The developed countries of Oceania are not immune from the scourge of poverty. Certain groups, particularly the indigenous peoples – the Aborigines in Australia and the Maori in New Zealand – tend to be poor. Although there are no longer laws that discriminate against indigenous peoples, it is taking a long time for them to catch up with the majority and to achieve a good education and decent jobs. According to Australia's 2006 census, Aboriginal people earned on average just under two-thirds as much as non-indigenous Australians.

Why are people poor and hungry?

As in sub-Saharan Africa, the state of the economy has the greatest impact on poverty levels. A large proportion of the population relies on farming for a living, so the international decline in prices paid for agricultural products since the 1980s has affected many people's incomes. Although economic development lifted many out of poverty during the 1990s and early 2000s, the recession of 2008 reversed some of the

This map shows the proportion of malnourished people in the countries of the Asia-Pacific region (2006).

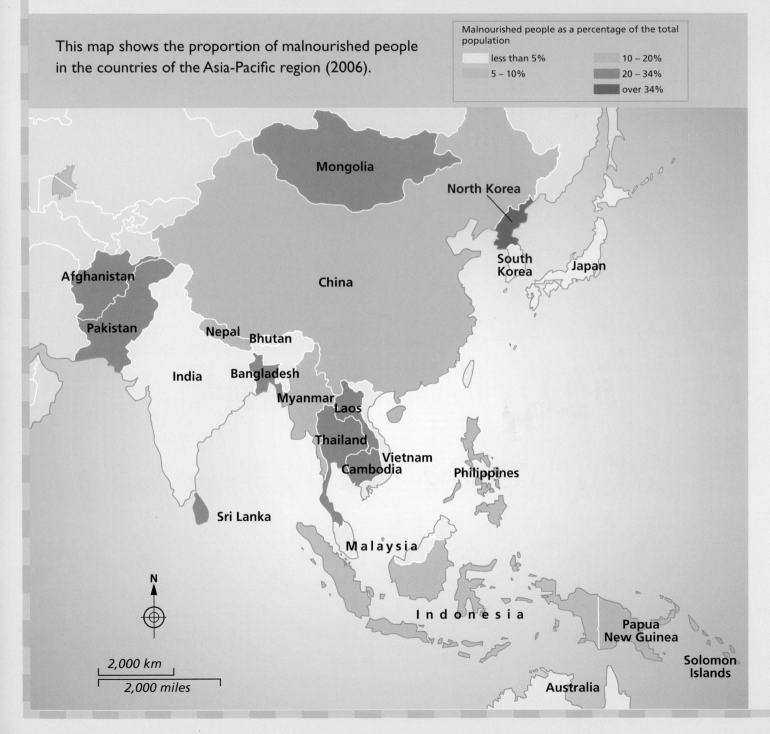

Malnourished people as a percentage of the total population

- less than 5%
- 5 – 10%
- 10 – 20%
- 20 – 34%
- over 34%

progress. Slower growth meant that fewer people escaped from poverty. The rise in food prices made matters worse; people who were already poor had to spend a larger part of their income on food.

Lack of welfare provision

Except for in Oceania, there is no 'safety net' to help people in economic difficulty. Only 20 per cent of jobless people in the region have access to unemployment benefits or training to assist them in finding a job. Only 30 per cent of older people receive pensions when they retire. These people have a greater than average chance of being in poverty.

Small babies, hungry children

South Asia has obstinately high levels of underweight children under five. A main cause is the low weight of babies at birth. Good child nutrition starts with the nutrition of the mother in pregnancy. If she is undernourished, her baby will be born underweight. Tiny babies are less likely to survive and develop properly.

Advances in reducing poverty

The Asia-Pacific region as a whole is on track to achieve the MDG to halve the number of people living below US$1.25 a day by 2015 (see page 9). The region has made more progress than sub-Saharan Africa but less than Latin America and the Caribbean. Yet it has been slow in reducing hunger.

CASE STUDY

KEEPING THE BABY SMALL

Gehold, a villager from Rajasthan, northern India, is typical of many poor Indian women. She is pregnant, and the doctor has advised her to drink milk and eat fruit. But she doesn't feel she can ask her family to spend money on expensive food just for her. Also, she needs to keep working as long as possible. Gehold said: 'I've been pregnant for four months now and my tummy is still small. This is good. I don't eat too much on purpose; I won't be able to bend if it gets too big. Then how will I work? The women here say that we should keep our babies small, so that we can keep working.'

Source: Save the Children website, 4 February 2008

The greatest advances have been made in the Asian Tiger countries of South-East Asia. As their economies have grown, they have achieved a rapid decline in poverty. Their governments have also invested in education and health care. Healthy people can hold down a job and work more efficiently, while educated workers can become skilled and access better jobs. These measures help to improve living standards while contributing to economic growth.

International aid

The governments of expanding economies can afford to invest in poverty-reducing measures. But what about the poorer countries of Asia? Such countries rely on aid, and this brings some benefits. In Bangladesh, for instance, international organizations are supporting a National Poverty Reduction Strategy, which aims to halve the number of poor people between 2005 and 2015. The plans include encouraging the private sector to expand and provide jobs, and involving the community in development projects. Yet aid does not always find its way to the people who need it most. In many cases it ends up in the pockets of corrupt officials. It is therefore important to ensure that these projects are properly implemented.

Local people, bright ideas

Anti-poverty schemes run by people within a country can be effective. The Grameen Bank is a micro-credit initiative in Bangladesh. It lends money to individuals so they can establish or improve small businesses. Once they are making a profit, they pay back the loan. In 2008, 65 per cent of the bank's 7.5 million borrowers managed to lift themselves out of extreme poverty.

Other simple methods can make the difference between starvation and survival.

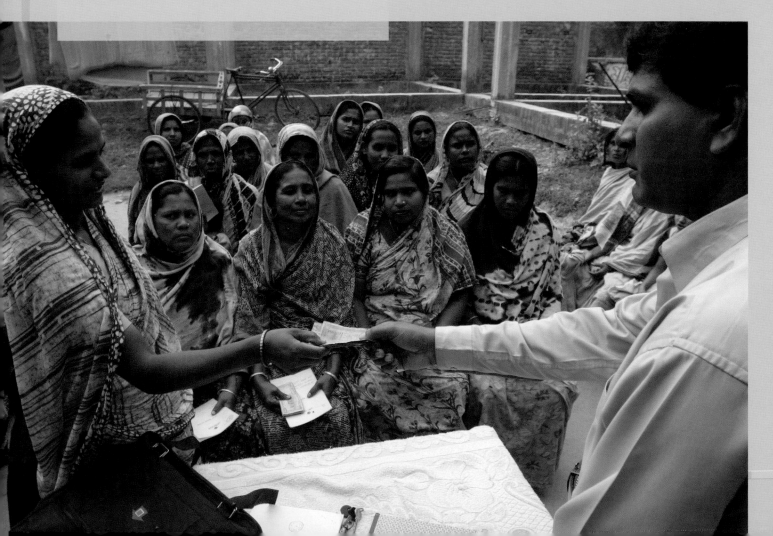

A woman receives a loan at the Grameen Bank weekly borrowers' meeting in Bariali, Bangladesh. Borrowers work together in groups to support each other and make sure that everyone repays their loan.

CASE STUDY

THE LADY LIVESTOCK WORKERS

In Pakistan, all fresh milk is produced by small domestic companies, so livestock training is an ideal way to enable women to run their own business. Razia is from a small village in the Punjab, Pakistan. After leaving her violent partner, she needed to find work to support herself and her child. She trained with the Livestock Development and Credit project, funded by the UK's Department for International Development (DFID), and qualified as a 'lady livestock worker'. She manages a milk collection centre in her village. The villagers supply milk to her and know they will be paid a good price, and promptly too. As well as making a decent living herself, Razia is training unemployed women in the village in livestock management.

Source: DFID website, 16 June 2009

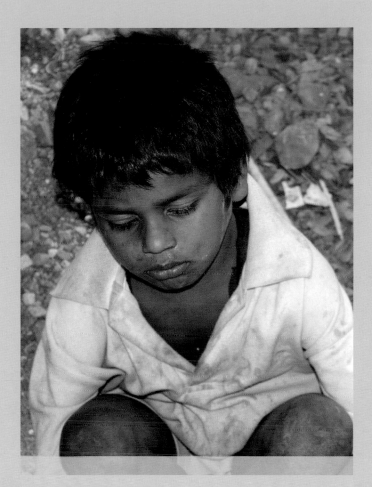

Anti-poverty schemes can help give children in India's slums the chance of a better future.

For example, Madhya Pradesh in India suffers from drought, and crop irrigation is essential. In the early 2000s, a local farmer developed the Pepsee drip irrigation system. He used the thin plastic piping usually used for Pepsee lollipops to make a network of irrigation pipes. Through the pipes, water is slowly and regularly applied directly to the roots of the plants, avoiding wastage.

Also of great use are businesses that offer valuable services to the poor at affordable prices. In India in the 1970s, businessman Bindeshwar Patkah pioneered low-cost public toilets in rural areas and overcrowded slums. In these places, homes had no toilets and people were forced to relieve themselves outdoors, causing serious hygiene problems. The toilets incorporate technology that can convert human waste into biogas, a fuel for cooking and producing electricity. In 2009, 1.2 million households used the toilets. Schemes like this can dramatically improve the lives of the poorest people.

4: The Middle East and North Africa

The Middle East and North Africa (MENA) region stretches from Morocco in the west to the western border of Pakistan in the east. In MENA, 17 per cent of people live on less than US$2 a day (2005). A huge disparity exists between the oil-rich Gulf nations and the poorest lands, such as Yemen, and between rich and poor within countries. This chapter looks at the issues of inequality and unemployment that affect this region, and the progress that has been made in reducing poverty.

It is hard to paint an accurate picture of poverty in MENA since several countries do not collect data. The figures can be confusing, too. Although the poverty rate is declining over the region as a whole, the number of poor people is increasing because of population growth. The proportion of the population living below US$1.25 a day fell from 4.3 per cent in 1990 to 3.6 per cent in 2005, but the total number increased from 9.7 million to 11 million.

FACTS and FIGURES

PERCENTAGE OF POPULATION LIVING IN POVERTY IN SOME MENA COUNTRIES

	ON US$2 A DAY	BELOW COUNTRIES' POVERTY LINE		
		Total	Urban	Rural
Algeria	15	23	15	30
Egypt	53	23	22	23
Jordan	7	12	10	18
Morocco	8	19	12	27
Tunisia	12	8	4	14
Yemen	n/a	25	22	27

* NOTE – people in rural areas are far more likely to be poor. Yemen is the poorest country.

Source: Population Reference Bureau, 2004

Where are people poor?

In general, the countries without oil resources are poorer. In Egypt and Yemen, poverty rates are more than twice as high as the average for the region. Yemen does have oil, but suffers from civil war, a badly managed economy and widespread corruption. The income from oil does not trickle down to the poor. In Egypt, poverty is particularly severe in rural areas; in Upper Egypt (the south) a shocking 45 per cent of children were in poverty in 2010. Many children, particularly girls, work to support their families and do not go to school. Therefore they are likely to remain poor when they grow up.

Causes of poverty: inequality

The major reasons for poverty are growing inequality, unemployment and the economic crisis. Owing to inequality, there are poor people even in the oil-rich countries. For instance, Saudi Arabia's vast oil riches have been used to help society to some extent by funding housing, transport, schools and hospitals. Yet a large proportion of the wealth is siphoned off by the ruling royal family, which enjoys lavish lifestyles at the country's expense.

Throughout the region, minority groups suffer unequal treatment that keeps them in poverty. For instance, in Lebanon there are 300,000 Palestinian refugees, mostly living in camps.

Palestinians are restricted from certain jobs and those who *are* employed do not benefit from Lebanese pensions or insurance plans. It was estimated in 2010 that 60 per cent of Palestinians were

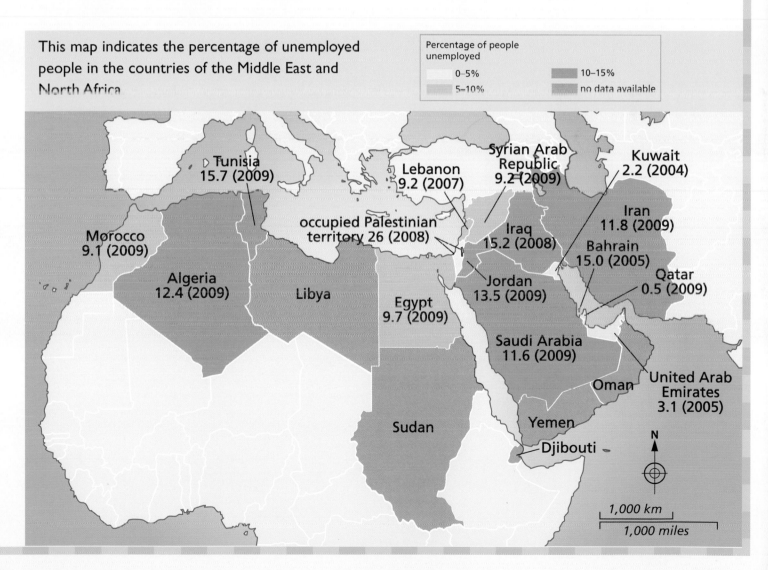

This map indicates the percentage of unemployed people in the countries of the Middle East and North Africa

Percentage of people unemployed

0–5%   10–15%
5–10%   no data available

Tunisia 15.7 (2009)

Lebanon 9.2 (2007)

Syrian Arab Republic 9.2 (2009)

Kuwait 2.2 (2004)

occupied Palestinian territory 26 (2008)

Morocco 9.1 (2009)

Iraq 15.2 (2008)

Iran 11.8 (2009)

Bahrain 15.0 (2005)

Algeria 12.4 (2009)

Libya

Jordan 13.5 (2009)

Qatar 0.5 (2009)

Egypt 9.7 (2009)

Saudi Arabia 11.6 (2009)

United Arab Emirates 3.1 (2005)

Oman

Sudan

Yemen

Djibouti

N

1,000 km
1,000 miles

unemployed. As 22-year-old Khaled, an electrical engineering graduate complained: 'I have been looking for over a year [for a job] with no success. I have been rejected because I am Palestinian, in spite of my credentials [suitability for the job].'

Economic growth – not all benefit

Even when an economy expands, the benefits do not trickle down to everyone in society equally. Rural dwellers, people in large families and those who are illiterate have a high chance of remaining in poverty. Economic downturns make the situation even worse – low-waged, casual workers are the first to lose their jobs. Generally in the region there is a lack of welfare provision for the poor, so people without work have to rely on their families to survive.

Inadequate education

An International Labour Organization report (2008) showed that MENA has the highest unemployment in the world. Education is usually the best passport to a good job. Surprisingly, although more people are receiving schooling, unemployment is high, especially among the young. A major cause of the problem is outdated education systems in the region. Students generally have to memorize answers to set questions rather than develop problem-solving skills, so they are not equipped with the skills needed by employers in the modern world.

Alleviating poverty

Income poverty is still a challenge in the region, although some countries are making progress towards the MDG goal to reduce extreme poverty and hunger. Iran and Tunisia saw a decline in the poverty rate between 2000 and 2010. MENA has done well in addressing other factors related to poverty – literacy and life expectancy have risen, while infant mortality has decreased. By 2000, the MENA region had caught up with many

middle-income countries, such as the Russian Federation and South Africa, for these indicators and it seemed probable that many MENA countries would achieve the MDG goal of universal primary education. Yet it is necessary to improve the quality of education to fit students for work.

Students take an exam at a school in Cairo, Egypt. The push to increase the numbers receiving education in Egypt has come at the cost of a dramatic fall in the quality of teaching.

5: The Americas

The Americas include Canada and the USA, Latin America (the Spanish- and Portuguese-speaking nations of Central and South America) and the Caribbean countries. Latin America and the Caribbean (LAC) have the region's highest levels of poverty. The causes of this are both economic and environmental. Yet poverty is not limited to the south. Even the United States, the richest nation on Earth, has large pockets of poverty.

Where life is hardest

The poorest countries are Haiti, Nicaragua, Bolivia and Honduras. Even before the devastating earthquake in Haiti of January 2010, more than a million of that country's 10 million people were so desperately poor that they depended on international food aid to survive.

Bolivia is one of the least developed countries in the region. In 2010 a massive 77 per cent of the rural population eked out their lives in poverty, and, on average, children attended school for just four years. The curse of hunger is greatest in the poorest countries. In 2009, 53 million people in LAC went hungry – about 9 per cent of the population.

The causes: plummeting prices

The main reasons for poverty are the effects of international trade, inequality within countries and environmental destruction. As in Africa and Asia, Latin American farmers depend on the sale of cash crops but have been hit by the downward spiral of prices for agricultural products. For instance, in

---

CASE STUDY

CHILD LABOUR IN BOLIVIA

In Bolivia about a third of children have to work to enable their families to survive. Ten-year-old Fiser harvests sugar cane alongside his mother in Bermejo. It is tough, physical work hacking the sugar canes with a machete (heavy knife) from dawn to dusk. Fiser's mother Angelica has been labouring in the fields since she was ten. She says of her son: 'He helps me a lot. He used to be at school but I need him to come to work with me, at least this year, then he can go back to school. Now we need the money so his little brothers can eat and go to school.'

Source: BBC News, Bermejo, 11 October 2009

This map of the United States compares the proportion of people existing below the poverty line in the different states.

Percentage of people living below poverty level

less than 11.0%
11.0–12.9%
13.0–15.9%
16 or more%

Alaska

Washington
Oregon
Idaho
Montana
North Dakota
Minnesota
Michigan
Wisconsin
Maine
Vermont
New Hampshire
New York
Massachusetts
Rhode Island
Connecticut
Pennsylvania
New Jersey
Delaware
Maryland
Nevada
Utah
Colorado
Nebraska
Iowa
Illinois
Indiana
Ohio
West Virginia
Virginia
California
Kansas
Missouri
Kentucky
North Carolina
Washington D.C.
Arizona
New Mexico
Oklahoma
Arkansas
Tennessee
South Carolina
Wyoming
South Dakota
Texas
Mississippi
Alabama
Georgia
Louisiana
Florida

Hawaii

Puerto Rico

the early 2000s, many coffee producers in Central and South America lost sales because coffee was being produced more cheaply in Vietnam. Also, the United States has flooded Latin American countries with cheap food exports. Local producers cannot compete on price and are forced to abandon their farms. Many Haitian farmers have gone out of business due to imports of cheap US rice.

The rich–poor divide

Inequality is another issue; Latin America has the widest gap between rich and poor of any region. A large part of each nation's wealth and income is concentrated in just a few hands. Also, whether people do well or not depends largely on circumstances outside their control: their race, gender, where they live and the level of their parents' education. If they belong to a group that endures discrimination, such as indigenous people in Colombia or Afro-Brazilians in Brazil, it is hard for them to improve their economic position.

Rich and poor in the United States

In contrast to its southern neighbours, the United States is wealthy. Yet the gulf between rich and poor has widened considerably since the 1970s. Then, chief executives of companies earned 30 times as much as the average worker. By 2007 they made nearly 300 times as much! In 2008 official figures showed that 13 per cent of Americans lived in poverty and 14 per cent lived in food-insecure households; they did not always have enough to eat. Malnutrition and obesity (being very fat) also result from poverty. The poorest people cannot afford healthy foods such as lean meat, fish, fruit and vegetables, while unhealthy, high-fat, processed foods such as biscuits and burgers are relatively cheap. American women on low incomes have a 50 per cent higher chance of being obese than those on high incomes.

Destroying the rainforests

The eating habits in rich countries, particularly the demand for meat, have led to increased poverty in poor countries. Huge swathes of rainforest in South America have been razed to the ground so that the

Volunteers at the Church of the Holy Apostle in New York serve over 1,200 hot, nutritious meals to homeless, unemployed and hungry clients every weekday.

A cattle ranch on former rainforest land in Brazil. Cattle farmers are able to expand into these areas because, according to Brazilian law, much of the rainforest is not owned by anyone.

land can be used for livestock farming and crops for animal feed. Rainforest has also been destroyed to grow biofuels for energy. This means less land is available for local people to produce food. In Brazil, a huge proportion – around 60 to 70 per cent – of deforestation (forest destruction) is carried out to create land for cattle ranches, leaving a far smaller portion that can be used for small-scale subsistence agriculture. Historically, subsistence agriculture did not harm the environment. Nowadays, there are so many people attempting to survive in a relatively small area of forest that the land cannot support them all.

As well as human-made destruction, the region is prone to natural disasters such as hurricanes, floods and earthquakes, which create massive environmental damage and exacerbate poverty. In turn, high levels of poverty make it harder to survive disasters. People in cheap, poorly constructed housing are extremely vulnerable to flood and earthquake damage. In the 2010 earthquake in Haiti, 300,000 people lost their lives and 1.5 million were left homeless when their homes were destroyed. Six months later, much of the damage had still not been repaired. The government could not afford to carry out the work, and much of the promised international aid had failed to arrive.

A helping hand from government

Some Latin American governments, for example, in Mexico, Brazil, Chile, Bolivia

---

FACTS and FIGURES

HAITI

Haiti is the poorest country in the western hemisphere.

- Population: 9 million.

- 80% live under the poverty line.

- More than two-thirds of the labour force are unemployed.

- Two-thirds of the population depend on agriculture, mostly small-scale farming.

- About half of the population lack an adequate clean water supply.

Source: Save the Children website, 2010

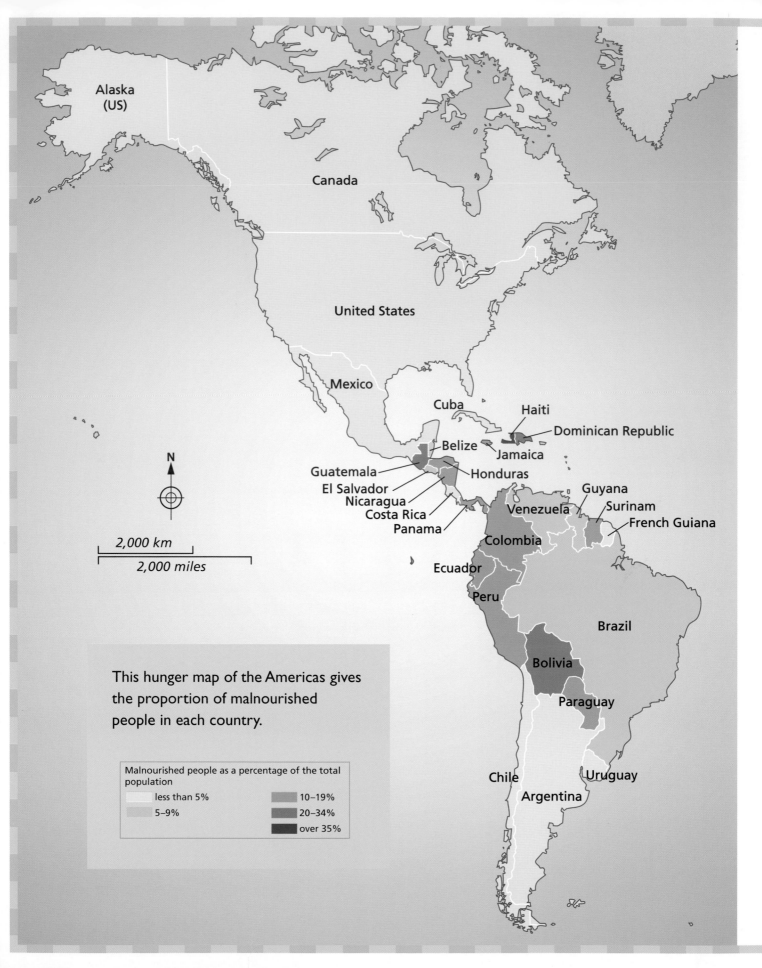

Alaska (US)

Canada

United States

Mexico

Cuba

Haiti

Dominican Republic

Jamaica

Belize

Guatemala

Honduras

El Salvador

Nicaragua

Costa Rica

Panama

Guyana

Venezuela

Surinam

French Guiana

Colombia

Ecuador

Peru

Brazil

Bolivia

Paraguay

Chile

Uruguay

Argentina

N

2,000 km

2,000 miles

This hunger map of the Americas gives the proportion of malnourished people in each country.

Malnourished people as a percentage of the total population

less than 5%

5–9%

10–19%

20–34%

over 35%

and Venezuela, have introduced social assistance programmes to tackle severe poverty. In Brazil the Bolsa Família scheme, started in 2003, provides cash transfers to extremely poor families. In return, they commit to sending their children to school and taking them for health checks. Promoting good health and education is the best way to improve the opportunities of the next generation. Similarly, in Bolivia, the Poverty Reduction Strategy allocates cash to poor families who keep their children in school.

In 2003 Venezuela established *misiones* – projects designed to end illiteracy and provide education, jobs, an electricity supply and health care to poor people. From the early 2000s the government promoted cooperatives, offering people training and support to set up and run their own enterprises. The government claims it has reached its MDG goal on poverty, having significantly reduced extreme poverty from 20 per cent in 1998 to 7.4 per cent in 2010 (official MDG sources had insufficient information to confirm these figures).

Grassroots movements

Initiatives do not only come from governments. Community groups may take matters into their own hands. The Landless Workers' Movement, set up in Brazil in 1985, occupies unused land and establishes cooperative farms. It has provided 1.5 million landless people with access to land and food security. The movement also encourages sustainable ways of living.

Giving some credit

Micro-credit schemes are a popular initiative in Peru, Colombia, Guatemala and Mexico and are spreading across the continent. For instance, in the desert town of Morrope, Peru, farmers struggle in the arid climate. A micro-credit scheme has allowed families to buy new livestock and seeds to plant a diverse range of crops suited to dry conditions, or even to build a well to irrigate their fields. A relatively small loan can make the difference between abject poverty and a comfortable living. From such small-scale programmes through to big government projects, some Latin American countries have achieved progress in shifting wealth towards the poorest in society.

6: Europe and Central Asia

This chapter will focus on the wealthy industrialized nations of Western Europe, some impoverished former Communist states in Eastern Europe and Central Asia, and many middle-income countries in between. The people who tend to experience poverty in this region are the unemployed, rural dwellers, the poorly educated, and minority groups that suffer discrimination. We will examine the areas where poverty hits hardest, the economic changes that have affected people's lives and efforts to improve living standards.

Which Europeans are poor?

In 2010, 40 million people in Europe and Central Asia (ECA) lived below US$2.50 per day (higher than the US$1.25 poverty threshold owing to the added cost of keeping warm in cold climates). Eastern European and Central Asian countries have the worst levels of absolute poverty and hunger. The poorest are Kyrgyzstan and Tajikistan, while Georgia and Uzbekistan have high poverty rates, too. However, the greatest number of the region's poor are in middle-income countries, such as Russia, Ukraine and Kazakhstan.

In the EU 15 – the 15 wealthy, Western European countries in the European Union – relative poverty has increased, exacerbated by the economic recession from mid-2008. Unemployment in the region reached

A beggar in Red Square in Moscow, Russia. The 2008–9 economic crisis caused a 30 per cent rise in the number of Russians living below the poverty line.

almost 10 per cent in 2010. Certain groups, such as the unemployed, sick or homeless, or people in large families, are more liable to become stuck at the bottom of the economic pile. Recent migrants usually receive lower pay than locals, as do young people, while retired people may also find it hard to make ends meet.

Roma children in the settlement of Zabjak, Slovenia, playing on the streets during school time. In some parts of Slovenia, Roma children do not attend school regularly.

CASE STUDY

THE ROMA: A CYCLE OF POVERTY

The Roma form the largest minority group in Eastern Europe. Owing to discrimination, they suffer from rundown housing, inferior schooling and a lack of decent job opportunities. For example, in Slovakia huge numbers of Roma children are wrongly sent to 'special schools' for people with mental disabilities. Up to 80 per cent of children in these schools are Roma. As one Roma boy, wrongly sent to a special school, explained: 'In grade 7 of the special school I learned the same things that I learned in grade 3 of the mainstream school.' The inadequate education these children receive makes it much harder for them to break out of the cycle of poverty.

Source: Amnesty International, 24 April 2009

Hungry and malnourished

The problem of hunger is most severe in the Caucasus and Central Asia, especially in Tajikistan, Armenia, Georgia and Azerbaijan. There were just under 6 million hungry people in Central Asia in 2004–6. Some people can afford to eat only one meal a day, and they eat a lot of bread rather than enjoying a balanced diet. Iodine and iron deficiencies are common, particularly in Georgia. These micro-nutrients are essential for children's growth. Iodine deficiencies can lead to mental retardation and brain damage. Pregnant women who are short of iron in the blood may give birth to small, weak babies.

Why is there poverty in Europe?

Between 1989 and 1991 the Communist governments of Central Asia and Eastern Europe collapsed. Before that, the governments controlled the economy and many aspects of their citizens' lives. People worked for the state rather than private companies. Virtually everyone had a job and a home, while good health, education and welfare services were provided by the government. After the Communist governments fell, there was a transition to a Western-style market economy. Some people benefited: they set up businesses, employed workers and made a profit. Yet many jobs disappeared when the economy was restructured, and job creation in new areas did not match the number lost.

The removal of welfare provision and the erosion of the state-provided health and education systems caused a dramatic rise in poverty in the former Communist region. At the start of the 1990s, less than one in 25 lived in absolute poverty. The figure rose to one in five in 1998. Economic growth in the early 2000s improved the situation, but the recession later in the decade reversed the advances. According to the World Bank, ECA was hit harder than any other region by the downturn. Poverty and joblessness increased. As Philippe Le Houérou, World Bank Vice President for the ECA Region, commented in 2010: 'Rising joblessness

FACTS and FIGURES

DEPRIVED IN EUROPE

- In 2008 the highest rates of deprived people who could not afford basic items were found in Bulgaria (51%) and Romania (50%). The lowest rates were in Luxembourg (4%) and the Netherlands and Sweden (5%).

- 37% of the EU 27 population could not afford a one-week annual holiday away from home.

- 10% could not afford to heat their home properly.

- 9% could not afford a meal with meat or fish every other day.

- 9% could not afford a car.

Source: Eurostat, January 2010

is pushing households into poverty and making things even harder for those already poor.'

The recession and hunger

The recession weakened the agricultural sector, slowing the drive to reduce hunger. Investment in agriculture is needed to improve technology and the infrastructure (such as transport) to cultivate more land and expand food production. This investment has not been forthcoming because of the downturn. Although the number of hungry people dropped significantly in the early 2000s, there were fears these gains would be reversed.

Not just the economy

The state of the economy has the greatest influence on poverty and hunger, but other factors also have an effect. Europe's population is rapidly ageing. People are having fewer children. There are more and more elderly people and a diminishing

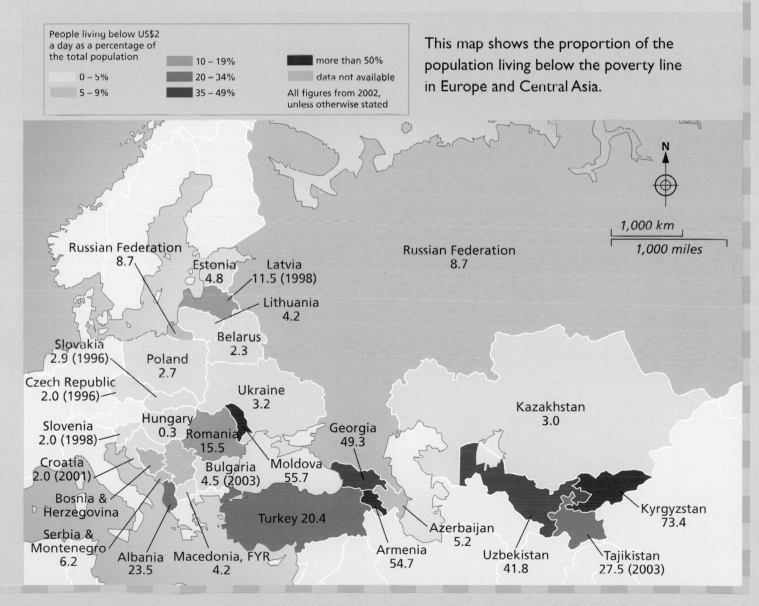

People living below US$2 a day as a percentage of the total population

- 0 – 5%
- 5 – 9%
- 10 – 19%
- 20 – 34%
- 35 – 49%
- more than 50%
- data not available

All figures from 2002, unless otherwise stated

This map shows the proportion of the population living below the poverty line in Europe and Central Asia.

N

1,000 km
1,000 miles

Russian Federation 8.7
Estonia 4.8
Latvia 11.5 (1998)
Lithuania 4.2
Belarus 2.3
Slovakia 2.9 (1996)
Poland 2.7
Czech Republic 2.0 (1996)
Ukraine 3.2
Slovenia 2.0 (1998)
Hungary 0.3
Croatia 2.0 (2001)
Romania 15.5
Georgia 49.3
Bosnia & Herzegovina
Bulgaria 4.5 (2003)
Moldova 55.7
Serbia & Montenegro 6.2
Albania 23.5
Macedonia, FYR 4.2
Turkey 20.4
Armenia 54.7
Azerbaijan 5.2
Uzbekistan 41.8
Russian Federation 8.7
Kazakhstan 3.0
Kyrgyzstan 73.4
Tajikistan 27.5 (2003)

number of working people to pay taxes and support them. Low pay is another issue – many people have a job but still live in poverty. In 2007, 8 per cent of EU 27 citizens in work were living below the poverty line. Economic growth in itself does not solve all these problems.

How governments are helping

National governments have introduced poverty reduction strategies to try to tackle poverty and hunger. Some of the worst-affected nations, such as Tajikistan, Kyrgyzstan and Moldova, have introduced policies to boost economic growth, improve technology and offer better public services. Some governments have targeted social assistance at the truly destitute. For example, in Kazakhstan in 2005 four-fifths of people who received benefits were unemployed or unable to work. However, the programme does not assist all poor people. It is complicated to apply for, which puts many people off. It can also create a 'poverty trap': it is not worthwhile for people on the programme to seek a job since they will lose their benefits and will not earn much more money by working.

Campaigns for higher wages

A way to address this issue is to raise pay levels. In Poland, for example, the two largest trade unions launched a campaign in 2007 for higher wages. They argued that low wages were a barrier to development;

many skilled workers were migrating to earn better money abroad. In the UK, the London Living Wage Campaign was launched in 2001 to fight for higher wages for the lowest-paid workers, such as cleaners and security guards, in this expensive city. By 2010 an estimated 25,000 people had been lifted out of poverty through living-wage policies agreed with employers.

Fighting poverty

Anti-poverty charities such as Save the Children, End Child Poverty and Oxfam equip people to help themselves. In Kyrgyzstan, for example, Save the Children enables disadvantaged children – girls, refugees, minorities, disabled children

PERSPECTIVES

NOT JUST FOR THE GOOD TIMES

Matthew Pennycook, the Campaigns Officer for the Fair Pay Network, UK, argues that if people are paid a fair wage – whether the economy is doing well or not – they are less likely to get into debt, which can tip them into poverty and harm the economy:

Fair pay policies are not just for the good times.... [We need a] model grounded in the principle that working people have a right to remain free from the blight of poverty and where adequate pay levels play their part in helping us move away from an economy built on the hazardous sands of unsustainable debt.

Source: Fair Pay Network, 2009

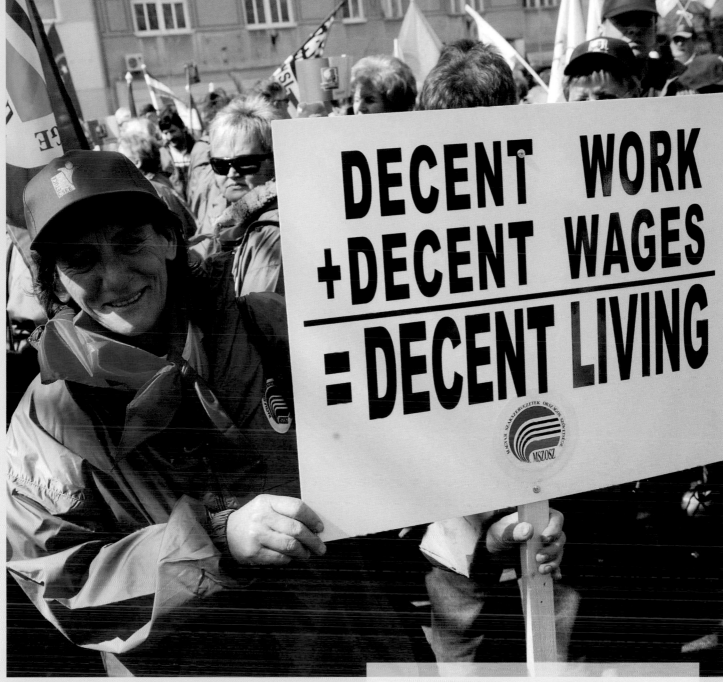

and orphans – to attend school. It assists street children who are scratching a living in Tajikistan's capital, Dushanbe. In the UK, the *Big Issue* provides an opportunity for homeless people to sell a magazine, earn an income and take some control of their lives. Government schemes, higher pay and

Around 30,000 European trade union members demonstrate in Ljubljana, Slovenia, for higher wages for workers, in 2008. Decent wages are a vital way to keep people out of poverty.

anti-poverty organizations can all help to eliminate poverty.

7: The Outlook for the Future

It is impossible to accurately predict future economic growth and its impact on reducing poverty. But a variety of policies could help, from fairer trade to cancelling poor countries' debt, more effective aid and improving the productivity of farming. Looking to the future, it is unlikely that the MDG to reduce poverty and hunger by half will be achieved across the globe by 2015. Climate change will present an immense challenge to food security, and efforts are urgently required to equip people to adapt to the new situation.

How can poverty be reduced?

Economic development increases a country's wealth and can reduce absolute poverty but may also increase the inequality between rich and poor. To lessen inequality, some experts recommend raising the taxes on richer people in order to improve services and benefits for the poorest. Yet others claim that this would affect wealthy people's incentive to invest in building businesses and creating jobs.

The best way to reduce the vast inequality between rich and poor nations is also fiercely debated. Some argue that globalization is the solution: expanding trade in world markets will help to lift poor countries out of poverty. Others maintain that globalization actually widens the gap. This is because the World Trade Organization, which fixes the trade rules, is dominated by wealthy countries. The rules favour those nations and disadvantage poor countries.

Fairer trade

Charities such as Oxfam argue that the trade rules should be fairer. Poor countries should not be forced to accept cheap imports from developed nations. Developing countries should be able to export to developed countries without paying high tariffs (export taxes). The international community could prevent the prices of basic agricultural goods such as rice, coffee and sugar from falling so low that producers can barely make any money from sales. On a small scale, the Fairtrade movement has implemented these suggestions, but even though one million producers and workers benefit from fairtrade, only a tiny proportion of agricultural products globally are fairly traded.

Drop the debt

Currently, the most heavily indebted countries pay far more in debt repayment than they receive in aid. The UK-based Jubilee Debt Campaign calls for the dropping of unjust debt – debts that a country cannot afford to repay if it is going to meet its people's needs. It also calls for the cancellation of debts to repay past loans to dictators or brutal regimes.

Target aid

To provide more assistance for poor countries, it would help if all the richer

These children attend a community school in Ipusukilo, Kitwe, Zambia. It was set up by a non-governmental organization for orphans and other children whose lives have been affected by AIDS. Education improves their chances of escaping poverty.

FACTS and FIGURES

AID VERSUS DEBT

The 10 countries that received the most Official Development Assistance in 2008, and the total foreign debt they owed (in US$ million).

	AID RECEIVED	DEBT OWED
1 Iraq	9,870	50,290
2 Afghanistan	4,865	2,700
3 Ethiopia	3,327	4,229
4 Palestinian Administrative Areas	2,593	1,300
5 Vietnam	2,552	31,000
6 Sudan	2,384	36,270
7 Tanzania	2,331	7,070
8 India	2,108	223,900
9 Bangladesh	2,061	23,220
10 Turkey	2,024	274,000

Source: OECD, 2010 and CIA World Factbook, August 2010

countries honoured their pledge to give 0.7 per cent of their national income in aid. Many observers argue that the aid provided could be focused more effectively on investment in basic services that can lift people out of poverty. Currently, some aid is spent on costly grand projects such as dam building, which do not assist the poorest people.

Reducing hunger

Low-cost, low-tech solutions can be extremely useful, such as assisting farmers in poor countries to increase agricultural productivity using high-yield seeds and fertilizers, and to make efficient use of water for irrigation. Farming needs to be sustainable – the nutrients should be restored to the soil to keep it productive. If farmers received higher prices for their produce, they could perhaps afford to return to growing some nutritious subsistence crops for themselves rather than devoting all their efforts to cash crops. As an interim solution, cost-effective nutrition measures could be provided for the malnourished, such as nutrient supplements for children and sick people.

Outlook for the future

In 2010 it was predicted that all the developing regions would meet the MDG target for reducing poverty, except for sub-Saharan Africa, Western Asia and parts of Eastern Europe and Central Asia. The world

poverty rate would fall to 15 per cent in 2015 – around 920 million people surviving below the international poverty line. However, climate change is expected to have a devastating impact on poverty and hunger over the next decades. In West Africa, lower rainfall is causing increasingly frequent droughts and the spreading of deserts, while low-lying regions, for example in Pakistan and Bangladesh, experience intense rainfall

CASE STUDY

COPING WITH CLIMATE CHANGE IN PAKISTAN

Some of the poorest people in Pakistan live in the coastal district, which used to be one of the biggest tomato-producing areas in Asia. Climate change has brought more intense rainfall, and sea water floods the land, making it too salty to grow crops. As 60-year-old Bhaagi says: 'In the old days (30 years ago), the land here used to be under cultivation, we grew wheat, tomatoes and watermelon. But now because of repeated flooding and heavy rains, and the cyclones [violent tropical storms], the seawater has intruded making the water brackish [salty] and leaving the land degraded, we can no longer grow anything.' Oxfam has started a project to protect the water supply and build embankments to defend villages from sea water. Using organic processes, the degraded land will be brought back into agricultural use to restore people's livelihoods.

Source: Oxfam, November 2009

and flooding. Projects can be developed to enable communities to adapt to climate change – if funding is available. Poverty and hunger will be reduced only if governments and international organizations make this a top priority and focus their efforts and resources towards this all-important goal.

Villagers collect food from a non-governmental organization after they were forced to leave their homes following a tidal wave in Sundarbans, India. Climate change appears to be making flooding more common in low-lying areas.

Glossary

absolute poverty When people do not have enough money to afford the basics, such as food, clothing and shelter.

biofuel A fuel made by biological materials, such as crops and animal waste.

cash crop A crop grown for selling rather than for use by the person who grew it.

Commonwealth of Independent States An association of states formed in 1991 by Russia and 11 other republics that had been part of the Soviet Union.

Communist To do with the system of government in the former Soviet Union, where the state controlled the production of goods.

cooperative A business owned and run by the workers, who share the profits.

debt relief Reducing the debts of a heavily indebted country so that it has more money for services such as education and health care.

deregulate Free a business activity from rules and controls.

developed countries Countries with many industries and a complex economic system.

developing countries Poor countries that are trying to make their industries and economic system more advanced.

drought A long period of time when there is little or no rain.

ethnic minority A group of people from a particular culture or race living in a country where the main group is from a different culture or race.

European Union (EU) An economic and political union of 27 member states – the EU 27. There have been 27 states since 2007. The EU 15 states are the member states as of 1995, before the Eastern European states joined.

fairtrade A partnership between producers in poor countries and consumers in rich countries, which allows producers to be paid a fair price for their products.

globalization The growth of international trade, communications, travel and culture since the 1980s.

grassroots movement A movement organized by ordinary people rather than governments.

indigenous Belonging to a particular place rather than coming to it from elsewhere. For example, the Aborigines are the indigenous people of Australia.

industrialize Develop industries on a large scale.

inequality A situation in which some people in society have more wealth than others.

interest rate Interest is the extra money that you must pay a lender when you borrow money. The interest rate is the rate at which the interest must be paid.

irrigate Supply water to an area of land so that crops will grow.

malnourished In bad health because of a lack of food or a lack of the right types of food.

micro-credit The provision of small-scale financial products and services, such as credits and insurance, to people on low incomes.

Millennium Development Goals Eight goals to reduce poverty, promote development and improve people's lives, which were agreed in 2000. The aim was to achieve the goals by 2015.

poverty line The official level of income needed to be able to afford the basic things people need, such as food, clothing and shelter. A person with less than this income lives in poverty.

privatizing Selling a business or industry to a company so that it is no longer owned by the government.

productivity The rate at which workers produce goods, compared with the time, work and money needed to produce them. High productivity means producing a large amount of goods cheaply in a short space of time.

recession A difficult time for the economy, when there is less trade and industrial activity and many people do not have a job.

relative poverty Being in poverty relative to others in your society so that you cannot afford items that most people have.

slum An extremely poor area where large numbers of people live, usually in low-quality housing without running water or sewerage facilities.

subsidy Money that is paid by the government to reduce the cost of producing goods so that their prices can be kept low.

subsistence agriculture Growing just enough food to live on.

transition countries Countries that used to be Communist states in the former Soviet Union and that started to move towards Western-style capitalism at the end of the 20th century.

transnational company (TNC) A corporation that manages production or delivers goods or services in more than one country.

Further Information

Books

Bono: *Fighting World Hunger and Poverty* by Mary-Lane Kamberg (Rosen Publishing Group, 2008)

Ending Poverty and Hunger by Judith Anderson (Franklin Watts, 2010)

Feeding the World by Sarah Levete (Heinemann, 2009)

World Hunger by Susan C. Hunnicutt (Greenhaven, 2006)

World Poverty by Sandra M Alters (Information Plus, 2008)

World Poverty by Sylvia Whitman (Facts on File, 2008)

Websites

www.oxfam.org.uk
Oxfam's Cool Planet: a website for young people about Oxfam's work in different countries, with a focus on children.

www.savethechildren.net
Save the Children's international campaign for children's rights, including the reduction of child poverty.

www.undp.org
United Nations Development Programme. This website has sections on the regions of the world and on poverty reduction.

www.un.org/millenniumgoals/poverty.shtml
United Nations Millennium Development Goals: a website with information about the MDG goals to eradicate extreme poverty and hunger.

Index